FLIP CHART POWER

Secrets of the Masters

BY BONNIE E. BURN

Pfeiffer
& COMPANY
INTERNATIONAL PUBLISHER
Johannesburg · London
San Diego · Sydney · Toronto

Interior Design and Illustration: Shana Lathrop
Cover Design: Susan Odelson
Page Compositor: Shana Lathrop
Technical Assistance: Ray Blavatt
Editor: Susan Rachmeler
Production Editor: Dawn Kilgore

Published by Pfeiffer & Company
8517 Production Avenue
San Diego, CA 92121-2280
United States of America

Editorial Offices: (619) 578-5900; FAX (619) 578-2042
Orders: USA (606) 647-3030; FAX (606) 647-3034

Printed in the United States of America

Printing 1 2 3 4 5 6 7 8 9 10
Library of Congress Cataloging-in-Publication Data
Burn, Bonnie
        Flip chart power / by Bonnie E. Burn
            p.   cm.
        ISBN 0-88390-485-3 (paper)
            1. Management—Charts, diagrams, etc.   I. Title.
HD38.B7946   1996
001.4'226—dc20

                                                                                95-53700
                                                                                CIP

Acknowledgments

A special thank you to these wonderful friends for their valuable professional insight and many kind words of encouragement.

Susan Murphy

Eunice Parisi

Maggie Payment

Marian Prokop

Susan Rachmeler

Rick Ten Eyck

Special note of thanks to two authors/experts in the field of flip charts, Richard Brandt and Lynn Kearny.

Contents

Part II Making Flip Charts

Part III Presenting Flip Charts

Appendix

Flip Chart Resources

Index

INTRODUCTION

Have you ever sat in a presentation or meeting and found your thoughts wandering to what you were going to have for lunch? This scenario is a good example of what can happen when an audience member is not involved.

The solution to this problem may surprise you: Flip charts. Yes, flip charts! You might ask "Aren't flip charts old fashioned? Non-high tech?"

And you would be right. Flip charts are not the most sophisticated visual aids available to presenters. However, flip charts are the visual aids most often used by presenters. Here are a few of the reasons why:

Flip charts are interactive tools. Flip charts promote audience participation and interaction. They are more user-friendly and less intimidating to audiences than other technologies. The mere appearance of a big piece of paper with large letters and colors tends to relax participants and ease their fears about saying anything. This leads to their being more active in providing you with ideas or problem-solving solutions.

Flip charts are effective visual aids that increase retention. Participants more easily remember concepts, ideas, or key points that are written down or symbolized by pictures.

Flip charts are versatile and can enhance many communication situations. There is ample space on a flip chart page to explain complicated concepts; conversely, you can use a page to highlight simple, very direct messages.

Flip charts are presented with the lights on, thus encouraging participants to stay alert. Having the lights on also helps to develop a connection between you and the participants: They can see your facial expressions and you can see their reactions.

Flip charts can be displayed on walls for easy reference. The sheets can easily be torn from the pad and taped to the walls. This allows the participants and you to refer back to previous material.

Flip charts are inexpensive. You need only a stand, flip chart pads, and markers.

Flip charts are easily produced. They don't require an artist or computer programmer to produce them: You just need time, space, and materials.

Flip charts and graphics are a natural combination. Flip chart pages provide plenty of space on which to draw graphics to explain or reinforce key points of your presentation.

Flip charts can be prepared quickly. Effective flip charts do not require fancy art-work. You can easily create flip charts yourself without having to hire and schedule a graphic designer.

Flip charts are not dependent on equipment or an electrical outlet to work. You need only enough space in which to position the flip chart stand. Flip charts also eliminate the stress of worrying about equipment breakdowns.

Flip charts can be taken anywhere. They can be rolled and transported without concern.

This book is designed to ensure that when you are the presenter, your participants will enjoy your session and find themselves actively involved. Professional trainers have been using flip charts for years to keep their audiences engaged while learning critical business skills. Flip chart techniques and methods are actually quite simple but make a powerful difference between flat presentations and winning presentations.

In the material that follows, you will learn many different uses for flip charts; the keys to making flip charts, including information about materials, preparation, and the best ways to incorporate graphics; and the secrets of effective flip chart presentation.

Flip Chart Power shares how professionals apply these approaches. This book will serve as a quick reference guide the next time you need to plan a presentation, session, or meeting of any kind.

Enjoy!

USING FLIP CHARTS

#1 GREETING PARTICIPANTS

FLIP CHART POWER

How To's

⁑ Be sure the flip chart faces the entrance of the room.

⁑ Use two bright, complementary colors.

⁑ Examples: green and black or blue and red

⁑ Write "Welcome to..." in large letters.

Situations

⁑ When beginning a session, regardless of topic.

Examples:
- For business meetings: "Welcome Managers"
- For team meetings: "Welcome Central Unit"
- For club meetings: "Welcome Members"

Advantages

⁑ Creates a positive, friendly first impression.

⁑ Assures participants that they are in the right place.

⁑ Helps participants and you feel more relaxed.

#2 PROVIDING INFORMATION

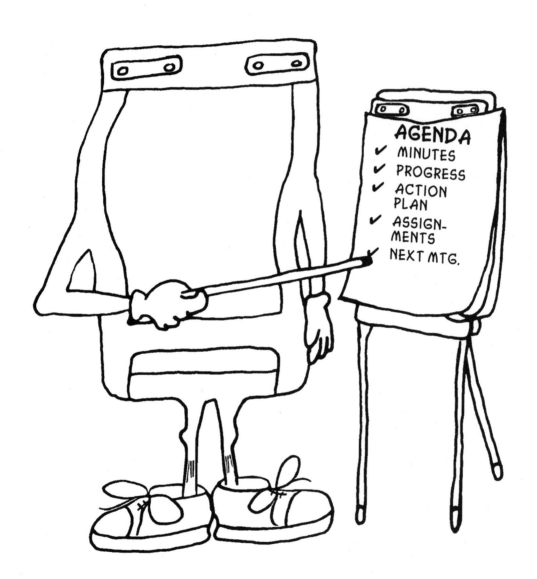

How To's

- Write the agenda on a flip chart before the meeting.
- Abbreviate words where appropriate.
- Limit copy to no more than 7 lines per page.

Situations

- When presenting course instruction (e.g., list the phases of adult learning).
- When presenting a topic outline.
- When trying to keep meetings on track and to maintain a time schedule.

Advantages

- Provides visual direction for the meeting.
- Encourages participants to give you their undivided attention (as opposed to staring down at paper agendas).
- Allows you to note agenda changes that then remain posted as visible reminders.

#3 Making Assignments

How To's

- Use this approach before you show a video.

- Write the question while participants watch.

- Write numerals instead of spelling numbers out.

Situations

- When participants are responsible for retaining information in an instructional setting.

- When you want participants to be more involved.

Advantages

- Builds suspense.

- Creates energy within the group by challenging participants to come up with the video's key points.

- Prompts participants to take the assignment more seriously.

#4 ASKING QUESTIONS

How To's

* Write the question before the meeting.

* Write the question on the top of the page, leaving plenty of space in which to write participants' responses.

* Write key words only.

Situations

* When you are conducting a group problem-solving session.

* When you need to get input from participants whose experience is critical to the success of the project.

Advantages

* Helps participants to stay focused on the topic.

* Encourages brainstorming because participants tend to want to fill up the space.

* Serves as an excellent, informal way to initiate problem solving.

#5 Recording Ideas

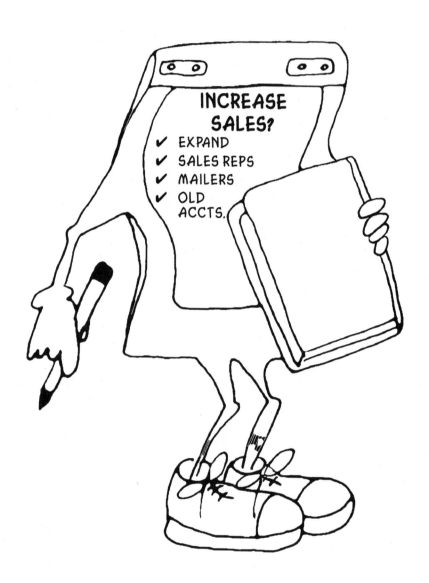

How To's

- Write participants' exact words; do not paraphrase.
- Abbreviate as needed to keep up with the group's ideas.
- Alternate colors between ideas.

Situations

- When you want to highlight or prioritize participants' responses.
- When you want to make sure that participants understand the ideas that have been presented.
- When you want to hold participants accountable for what they have said they will do.

Advantages

- Shows that you value participants' input.
- Encourages participants to suggest ideas.
- Gives participants visual cues as to where one idea ends and another begins.

#6 Displaying Content

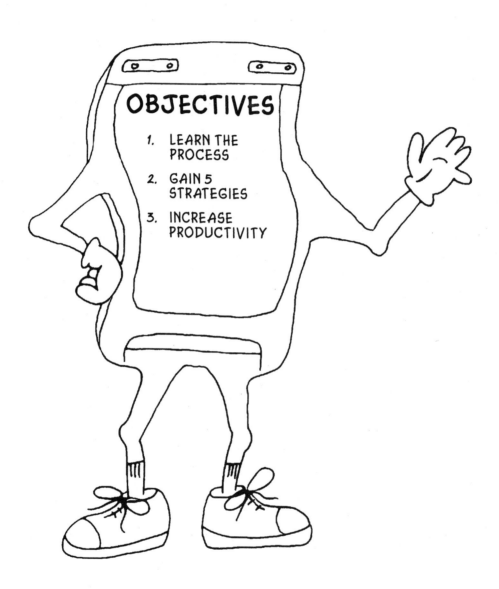

Within the illustration:

OBJECTIVES

1. LEARN THE PROCESS

2. GAIN 5 STRATEGIES

3. INCREASE PRODUCTIVITY

How To's

≢ Select the content that you want to emphasize throughout the session.

≢ Post flip charts on the wall in a row.

≢ Hang flip charts no more than 6 feet from the floor. (Remember, participants are sitting down when they are viewing your flip chart.)

Situations

≢ When you need to be able to refer to previous points with ease.

≢ When you are summarizing the content of your presentation or reviewing agreed-on action plan steps at the end of the session.

Advantages

≢ Keeps the focus on the key points.

≢ Can be used to display other content as well: schedules, models, processes, or charts.

#7 Transforming a Concept into a Picture

How To's

≋ Objects (concrete words) are specific and physical.

Examples: phone, ladder

≋ Select an object to represent
the concept you want to discuss. Make sure that the association is
one that participants can grasp.

Examples:

* Concept is communication (object is phone)

* Concept is progress (object is ladder)

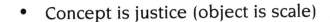

* Concept is justice (object is scale)

Situations

≋ When you want to explain a concept
(e.g., establishing rapport with a
customer).

≋ When you want to explain an abstract
concept in tangible form (e.g.,
excellent customer service).

Advantages

≋ Helps participants to
remember abstract ideas.

≋ Allows you to include more variety in your presentation.

#8 Reviewing Ideas

PLAN 1
- ✔ TRAIN ON THE JOB
- ✔ PERF RVW-1 MO.
- ✔ PERF RVW-2 MOS.

PLAN 2
- ✔ ATTEND SEMINAR
- ✔ WRITE REPORT
- ✔ USE AT WORK

PLAN 3
- ✔ WATCH VIDEO
- ✔ TAKE TEST
- ✔ DISCUSS RESULTS

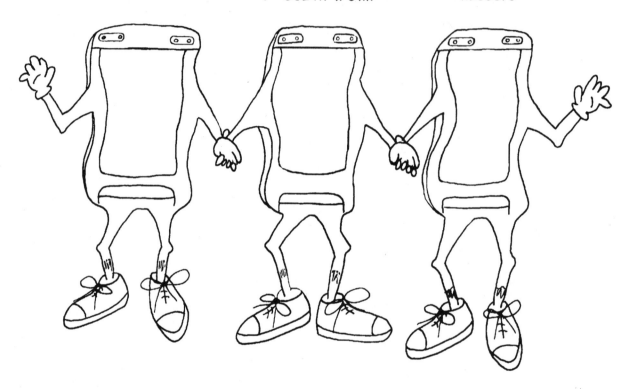

How To's

≋ Record participants' responses.

≋ Rip off each flip chart page when completed.

≋ Tape flip chart pages to the wall during a break or when participants are doing some type of group activity.

≋ Hang flip chart pages so participants can see them easily.

Situations

≋ When responding to a participant who asks a question or challenges you. (You can refer back to the flip chart page that helps explain your answer.)

≋ When you are presenting many points and need to show the connection or linkage between them.

Advantages

≋ Reinforces to participants the idea that their responses will be the basis for decision making.

≋ Encourages commitment from participants.

≋ Provides an overall view of all the options that were discussed.

#9 SETTING PRIORITIES

VOTE
TALLY

PLAN 1 - 10

PLAN 2 - 4

PLAN 3 - 12

How To's

 ⚡ Use one of the following polling options to determine priorities:
  • Ask participants to raise their hands to vote for the plan they prefer.
  • Have each participant come up to the flip charts and place a mark beside the plan he or she prefers.

Situations

 ⚡ When participants need to decide on a course of action.

 ⚡ When making decisions based on the participants' ideas and concerns.

Advantages

 ⚡ Helps to move a problem-solving process to the decision-making stage.

 ⚡ Shows participants how priorities are being identified, adding credibility to presentation.

 ⚡ Encourages the group's commitment to the project.

#10 Highlighting Points

How To's

- Have each team present its recommendations.
- Comment on the ideas that are exceptionally good.
- Circle the exceptional ideas in a bright, contrasting color.

Situations

- When you want participants to be able to focus easily on the most important topics, points, or skills.
- When you need to get participants' attention amid distractions.

Advantages

- Provides immediate feedback to participants.
- Helps participants focus visually on the best ideas.
- Encourages participants to continue giving input.

#11 RESTATING IDEAS

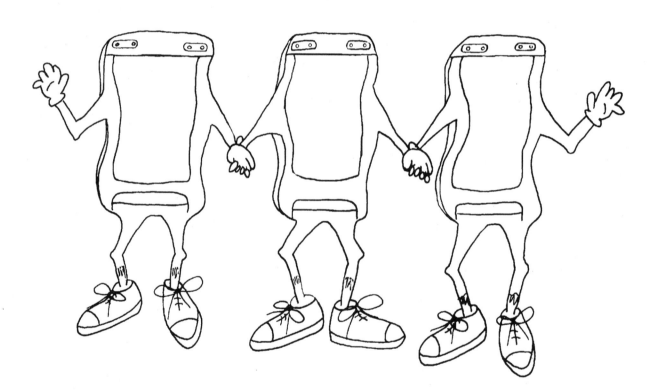

TEAM 1

RESOURCES:
- ✔ LIBRARY
- ✔ ASSOC.
- ✔ TRADE SHOW

TEAM 2

RESOURCES:
- ✔ YELLOW PAGES
- ✔ INTERVIEWS
- ✔ CONVENTION

(NEW CHART)

KEY RESOURCES:
- ✔ TRADE SHOW
- ✔ CONVENTION

FLIP CHART POWER

How To's

⚡ Write the topic title at the top of a new flip chart.

⚡ Transfer the exceptionally good ideas you circled to the new flip chart.

Situations

⚡ When you want to ensure clear communication with participants about what has been decided during the session.

⚡ When you want to underline a particular point (e.g., a new policy that must be implemented immediately).

Advantages

⚡ Focuses attention on the key ideas.

⚡ Demonstrates the importance of participants' good ideas.

⚡ Helps participants to see the next step more clearly by eliminating or postponing less important ideas.

#12 Revealing Information

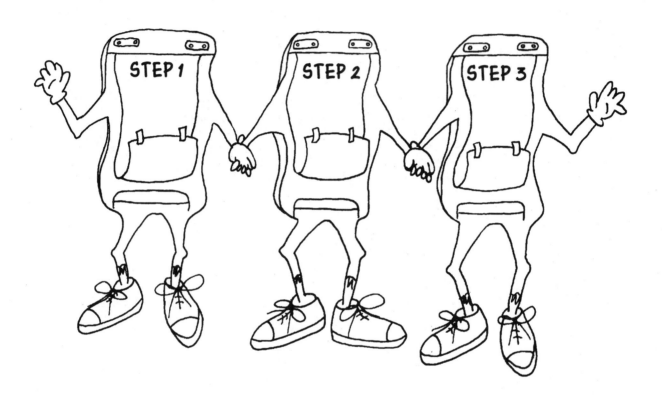

How To's

≋ Prepare and display the flip charts in sequential order before the training session.

≋ Fold and tape the bottom of each flip chart up so that only the title of each flip chart is showing.

≋ Reveal the hidden information at the appropriate times during your presentation.

Situations

≋ When you want to help participants to focus on one piece of information at a time.

≋ When you want to create intrigue and arouse curiosity.

Advantages

≋ Helps build anticipation by concealing information from participants at the beginning.

≋ Enhances learning by allowing you to reveal the content as building blocks, a step at a time.

#13 Organizing to Increase Retention

ORGANIZING

✔ WORDS &
  IMAGES
✔ RETENTION

How To's

🖋 Identify the key parts of the concept you are presenting.

🖋 Select 1 to 5 words and an image to represent each part to clarify
   the meaning of the concept.

Example:
- If the concept is the communication process, then the flip chart might look like the following:

COMMUNICATION PROCESS

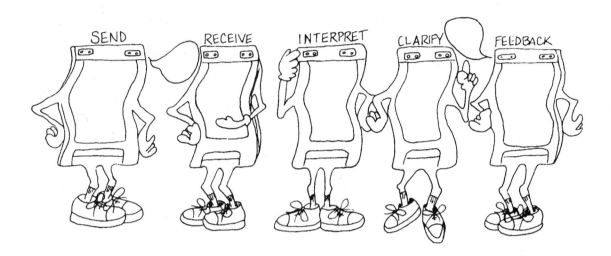

SITUATIONS

≋ When you want to present complex, detailed, or new concepts in a simple manner.

≋ When you want participants to remember key components of your topic.

≋ When you want participants to see the logical sequence of the larger concept.

ADVANTAGES

≋ Well organized flip charts are interpreted accurately, learned rapidly, and remembered.

≋ Using words and pictures to present complex concepts or detailed processes makes it easier for participants to remember the key points.

#14 Making Action Plans

HIRING		
TASK	WHO	BY
REVISE JOB DESCRIPTION	MGR	10-5
TURN IN TO H/R	MGR	10-12
FILL OUT REQUISITION	MGR	10-13
AD COPY WRITTEN	HR DEPT	10-15
SUBMIT AD COPY	HR DEPT	10-17

How To's

‡ Ask participants to list the tasks necessary to achieve the objective.

‡ Rewrite the list in sequential order on another flip chart.

‡ Add who is responsible for accomplishing each task and by when the task should be completed.

Situations

‡ When you need to keep a group on track with a specific objective.

‡ When trying to build accountability in a group.

‡ When assisting a group to begin implementing or accomplishing a task or project.

Advantages

‡ Pins down, in writing, what steps need to be taken to achieve the objective.

‡ Helps clarify who will do a task and assures all participants that someone is accountable for each task.

‡ Increases the odds that the project will be completed on time.

#15 Reviewing Material

How To's

⚡ Test retention with one or more of the following options:
- An individual assignment: Have each participant work on his or her own. After each participant has had time to think about the answers, conduct a discussion about the answers.
- A team assignment: Divide participants into teams. Give each team a newsprint pad or flip chart and have members work together to come up with the answers.
- A team competition: After each team has completed its flip chart, ask teams to trade flip charts and grade one another's work.

⚡ Any of these options can be done as an open-book test (usually if review is quite technical).

⚡ List the correct answers on the flip chart.

Situations

⚡ When trying to determine how well participants have grasped the new concepts, skills, or guidelines.

⚡ When you want to measure participants' receptivity.

⚡ When you need to provide supervisors or management with a report.

Advantages

⚡ Helps to increase participants' retention.

⚡ Creates a more relaxed learning environment when done in teams.

⚡ Reinforces the benefit participants will receive from their notes and handouts in the future.

#16 Making Simultaneous Team Assignments

How To's

- Have the topic assignment already written at the top of each flip chart.

- Give both teams the same assignment and a flip chart.

- Present, in turn, each team's ideas.

Situations

- When you want to expand participants' openness to new ideas.

- When you want to tap into participants' expertise and resources.

- When you want to challenge participants by using a competitive team format.

Advantages

- Creates a sense of teamwork for each team.

- Allows participants to hear other participants' ideas, which they may be more open to than your ideas.

- Provides the opportunity for participants to see what another team develops.

#17 MAKING DIFFERENT TEAM ASSIGNMENTS

How To's

🌿 Identify and list each discussion topic on a separate flip chart before the session.

🌿 Write only the key words that describe that topic.

🌿 Divide participants into teams and give each team a different flip chart.

🌿 Ask each team to come up with as many responses as possible.

🌿 Have a team leader present the team's ideas.

Situations

🌿 When you want to explore an idea from many angles.

🌿 When you need to cover a lot of material in a short period of time.

Advantages

🌿 Gives clear direction to participants and helps them to stay focused.

🌿 Allows you to cover more material in less time.

🌿 Reduces redundancy in the ideas that are generated.

#18 FOCUSING EMPHASIS

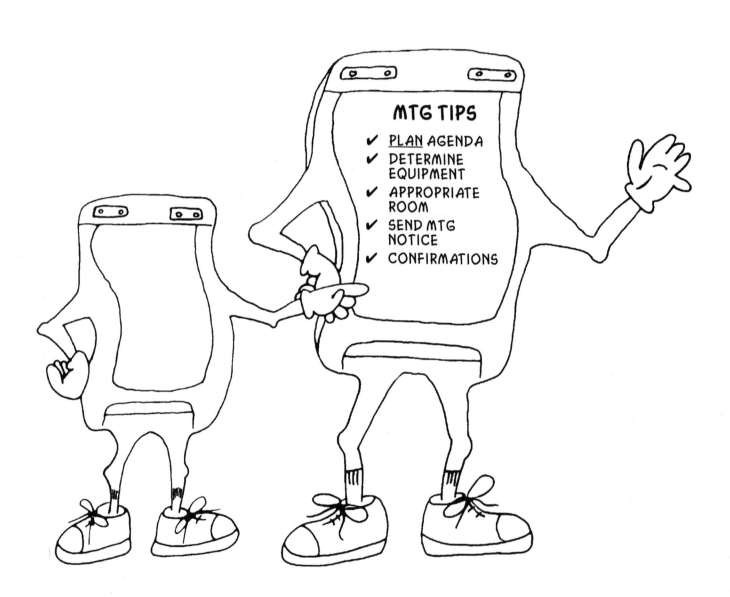

How To's

☙ List information on a flip chart before the session.

☙ Underline, circle, or put stars next to the item to be emphasized.

☙ Use a bright, contrasting color for emphasis.

Situations

☙ When you want to ensure that participants have grasped the important points of a subject, process, or concept.

☙ When questions continue around a particular issue, go back to that flip chart page and emphasize the appropriate content.

Advantages

☙ Provides a complete picture as well as allowing you to focus on the area that requires more attention.

☙ Indicates the topic you want to discuss next.

#19 DIRECTING ATTENTION

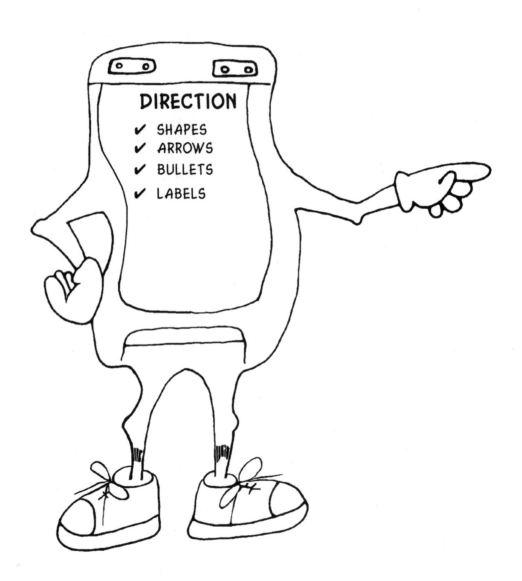

How To's

- Use bullets, shapes, and arrows to direct participants' attention.

Bullets:

■ Square　　　▲ Triangle　　　● Dot

Shapes:

Frames	⬭ Ovals	Clouds	Circles
Hold Attention	Gather Attention	Draw Attention	= Bull's-eye ◉

Arrows:

Direct Attention　　‖‖‖➡

- Write key words to explain the specific item to which you are referring.

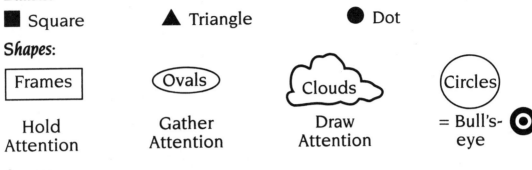

WHEEL

Situations

- When emphasizing or underscoring a particular point.

- When transitioning from one topic to another.

Advantages

- Helps to direct participants' attention to important information.

- Helps to clarify how a process flows or a program functions.

#20 Filling In Answers

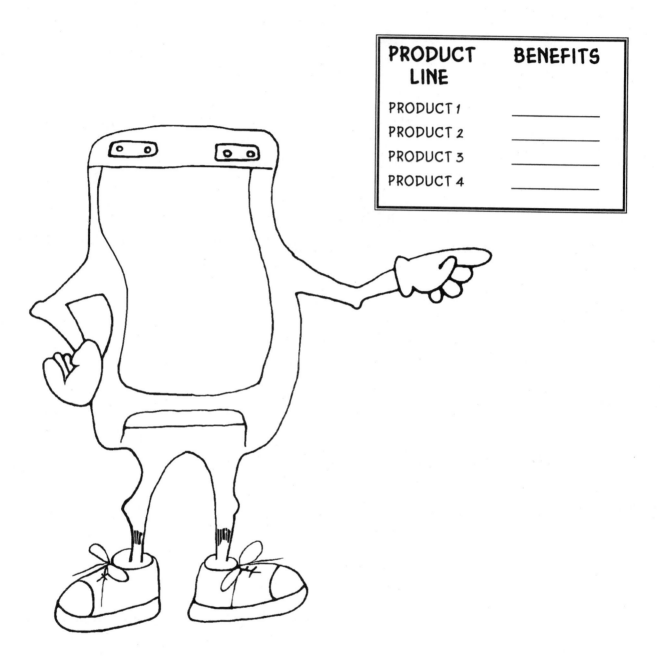

PRODUCT LINE	BENEFITS
PRODUCT 1	_____
PRODUCT 2	_____
PRODUCT 3	_____
PRODUCT 4	_____

FLIP CHART POWER

How To's

≋ Write the topic title and the first column of information before the session.

≋ Use the same color for the title and the first column of information.

≋ Ask participants to call out their answers.

≋ Write their answers in the second column in a bright, contrasting color.

Situations

≋ When testing participants' knowledge level on content that you just presented.

≋ When you want to help trigger participants' memory of key points, especially if you have presented a lot of content.

Advantages

≋ Helps to jump start discussion by providing half of the information.

≋ Alleviates participants' intimidation if some of the information is already provided.

≋ Takes less time to get key information across to participants.

#21 Posting Discussion Questions

How To's

- Ask only relevant questions.

- Ask questions that require more than a one word answer (open-ended questions).

- Ask questions that participants can most likely answer from their own experience.

Situations

- When you need to determine the existing knowledge level of participants on your presentation topic. You can then adapt your presentation accordingly.

- When participants have some knowledge about or experience with the topic and you want to get their input and feedback.

Advantages

- Helps to get participants involved in the topic immediately.

- Draws on participants' knowledge about the topic.

- Shows how the session will benefit participants.

#22 Interjecting Humor

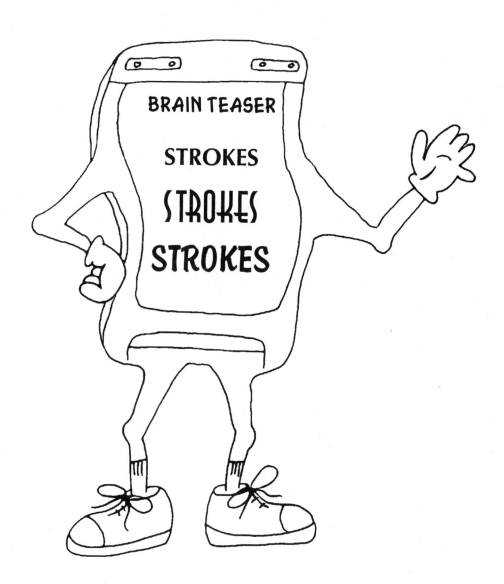

ANSWER: DIFFERENT STROKES

How To's

- Put the puzzle on a flip chart before the session.
- Choose something directly related to the topic if you're using it as part of your presentation.

Situations

- When conducting any type of presentation, if humor is appropriate and in good taste.
- When you want a visual break at the beginning of a unit.

Advantages

- Provides an easy way to change pace in a presentation.
- Helps to lighten the mood if the session topic is a particularly heavy or tense one.
- Can portray easily a concept that may otherwise require a lot of explanation.

#23 Giving Instructions

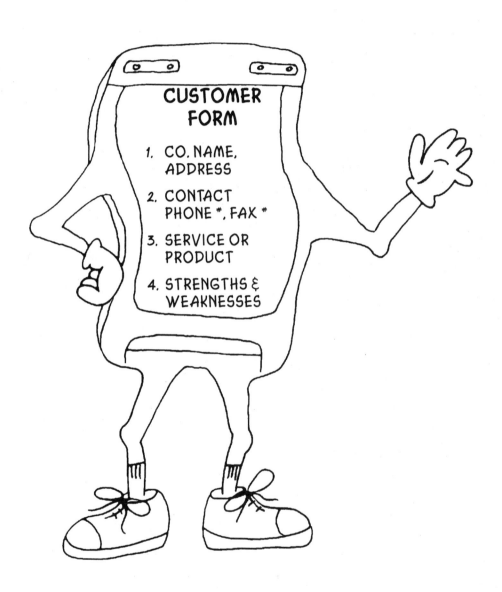

How To's

* List the topic and the steps in sequential order on a flip chart before the session.

* Use alternating colors to list the steps.

* Keep instructions to a minimum on the flip chart. If more detail is needed, provide an additional handout with more particulars.

Situations

* When communicating your expectations of the participants.

* When participants' performance depends on understanding and implementing your instructions correctly.

Advantages

* Assists participants in clearly understanding the order in which the steps should be completed.

* Demonstrates that you are well organized, thus encouraging participants to take session more seriously.

#24 BRAINSTORMING IDEAS

How To's

- Ask participants to respond with ideas.

- Tell participants that all ideas are acceptable.

- Write participants' exact words, but abbreviate as needed.

- Complete the process by setting priorities, highlighting points, restating ideas, and making action plans.

Situations

- When you want to incorporate a new method for group problem-solving.

- When helping a group break out of routine ways of thinking.

Advantages

- Encourages more involvement by letting participants know that all ideas are acceptable.

- Demonstrates that you respect participants' expertise and knowledge about the topic.

- Provides a visual record of ideas.

- Gives each participant an opportunity to voice an opinion, thus encouraging commitment.

#25 Reserving Discussion

How To's

≉ List the content to review with participants on the first flip chart; write only "Concerns" on the second flip chart.

≉ Record participants' concerns on the second flip chart as they arise, using their exact words.

≉ Inform participants that their concerns will be discussed after the first part of the program is completed.

≉ Discuss concerns at the session's end.

≉ Set up action steps that will help address these concerns.

Situations

≉ When a participant has raised a point that is not relevant to the topic at hand.

≉ When a very controversial point is being discussed and no progress is being made.

≉ When you do not have sufficient time at the moment to deal with a valid participant concern or point.

Advantages

≉ Allows you to stay focused on the main thrust of your session while providing an outlet for participants to voice concerns.

≉ Helps to ease tension.

≉ Works toward getting involvement from participants who might otherwise get preoccupied with a concern.

#26 Making Complex Ideas Simple

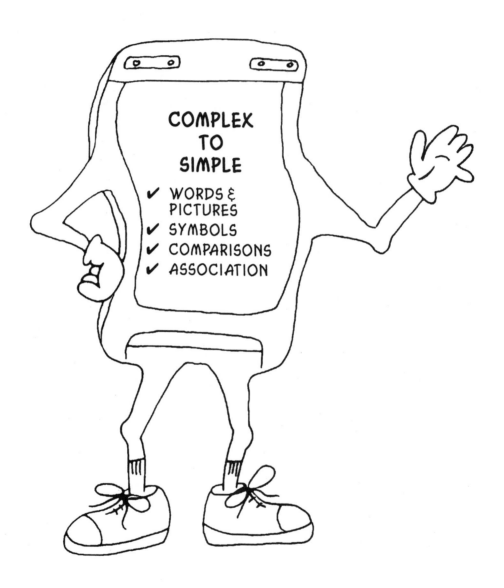

How To's

     ≋ Combine a picture and a word (label).

       Example:

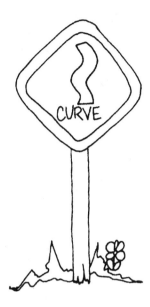

     ≋ Combine boxes, symbols, and arrows.

       Example:

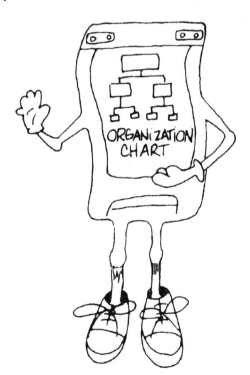

≝ Position items next to one another so that comparisons can be made.

Example:

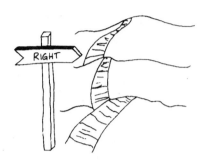 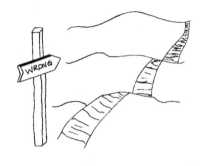

Right Way vs. **Wrong Way**

Situations

≝ When presenting a flow chart.

≝ When explaining the steps in a process.

≝ When showing the relationship between two items.

Advantages

≝ Allows participants to grasp complex ideas quickly by associating them with simple images.

≝ Works well for illustrating processes.

≝ Provides a graphic way to give instructions.

KEY POINTS

Purpose

Decide what it is that you are trying to accomplish.

Applications

Choose flip chart applications that are appropriate for your purpose, whether it be informing, instructing, eliciting feedback, brainstorming, problem solving, changing the pace, adding levity to a tense situation, enhancing teamwork, guiding discussions, or reinforcing a topic.

Pre-drawn and Spontaneous Flip Charts

Preparing flip charts before the session (pre-drawn) adds credibility to your presentation. Writing on flip charts during the presentation (spontaneous) encourages more involvement from your participants. And, of course, you can combine the two styles for maximum advantage.

QUICK CHECK

Instructions: Match the flip chart application in the left column with its advantage in the right column.

APPLICATIONS

Giving
Instructions

Recording
Ideas

Reserving
Discussion

Making
Action Plans

Brainstorming
Ideas

Reviewing
Ideas

Revealing
Information

Transforming a
Concept into a
Picture

ADVANTAGES

Gives all participants an opportunity to voice an opinion, encouraging commitment.

Helps participants to remember abstract ideas.

Pins down, in writing, what steps need to be taken to achieve the objective.

Shows that you value participants' input and encourages others to suggest ideas.

Enhances learning by allowing you to present content as building blocks, a step at a time.

Provides an overall view of all the options that were discussed.

Assists participants in clearly understanding the order in which the steps should be completed.

Works toward getting involvement from participants who might otherwise get preoccupied with a concern.

NOTES

Quick Check Answers

APPLICATIONS	ADVANTAGES

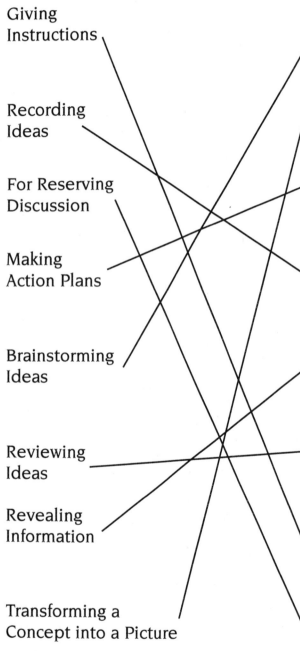

Giving
Instructions

Recording
Ideas

For Reserving
Discussion

Making
Action Plans

Brainstorming
Ideas

Reviewing
Ideas

Revealing
Information

Transforming a
Concept into a Picture

Gives all participants an opportunity to voice an opinion, encouraging commitment.

Helps participants to remember abstract ideas.

Pins down, in writing, what steps need to be taken to achieve the objective.

Shows that you value participants' input and encourages others to suggest ideas.

Enhances learning by allowing you to present content as building blocks, a step at a time.

Provides an overall view of all the options that were discussed.

Assists participants in clearly understanding the order in which the steps should be completed.

Works toward getting involvement from participants who might otherwise get preoccupied with a concern.

MAKING FLIP CHARTS

Paper

COMMON PAPER

✔ WHITE PAD: 27" X 34"
✔ BLANK OR GRID
✔ 60 SHEETS
✔ HOLES AT TOP

COMMON PAPER

✔ NEWSPRINT PADS: 12" X 18" OR 18" X 24"
✔ 100 SHEETS
✔ SPIRAL BOUND AND/OR PERFORATED

TIPS

❧ Purchase flip chart pads, newsprint pads, or binders at office and art supply stores.

❧ Grid-lined flip charts are the most practical. Grids are subtle and help you print in a straight line. The grids also help you line up margins, subheadings, and bullets, and create balance in the flip chart.

❧ Use a yardstick to lightly draw pencil lines on blank flip charts.

❧ Make a flip chart page filled with rows of black marker lines. Use this as a template behind a blank flip chart page. The lines will guide your printing, and the template page will absorb any ink that might bleed through to the next flip chart page.

Markers

POPULAR MARKERS
- ✓ PERMANENT
- ✓ WATER COLOR
- ✓ SET OF 12 BRIGHT COLORS
- ✓ CHISEL TIP
- ✓ SCENTED

Tips

- Purchase markers at office and art supply stores, discount stores, or grocery stores.

- Markers come in different sizes, shapes, and types of points.

- Permanent markers' colors are darker; blacks are black, not a dark gray. They have a strong smell of ink.

- Water color markers do not bleed through to the next flip chart page and will wash out of clothing.

- A fun way to start a meeting is to have participants write their name badges with bright, scented markers (red, magenta, blue, green, dark green, turquoise, pink, orange, purple, brown, black). A popular brand for water color scented markers is "Mr. Sketch"® by Sanford.

Tape

DEPENDABLE
TAPE
✔ GENERAL
  PURPOSE
  MASKING
  TAPE
✔ 1" WIDTH,
  60 YD

Tips

- Purchase tape at office and art supply stores, discount stores, or grocery stores.

- Be sure to test the wall in a low, inconspicuous location. Some tape takes the paint off the wall.

- If you purchase a brand of masking tape other than Scotch™, be sure to check its ability to hold a flip chart page for several hours. It is very frustrating and distracting to have flip charts falling off the walls while you are trying to make an important point.

- Some surfaces do better with stick pins, straight pins, magnets, clips, or drafting tape.

Stand

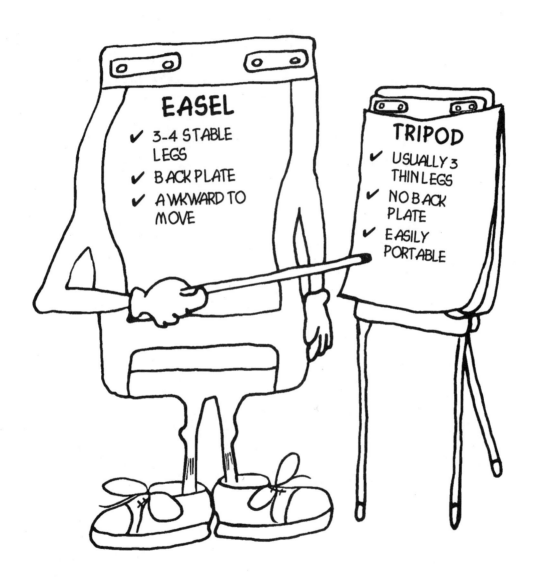

Tips

≉ Purchase easels and tripods at office and art supply stores.

≉ Easels and tripods can be constructed of wood or metal.

≉ Most easels and tripods are capable of holding at least one full pad of flip chart paper (approximately 60 sheets).

≉ Some easels and tripods have legs that can be telescoped so that a desktop version of a flip chart stand can be produced.

≉ Easels and tripods with pins for hanging flip charts are easier to manage than ones with clamps.

≉ Trays are available that can be attached to an easel to hold markers.

Survival Kit

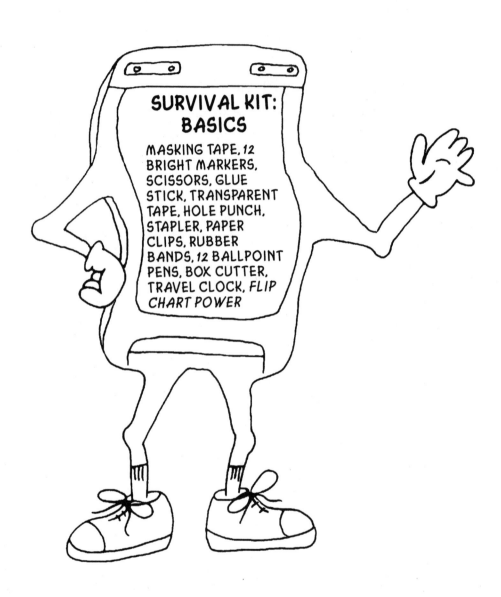

SURVIVAL KIT:
BASICS

MASKING TAPE, 12
BRIGHT MARKERS,
SCISSORS, GLUE
STICK, TRANSPARENT
TAPE, HOLE PUNCH,
STAPLER, PAPER
CLIPS, RUBBER
BANDS, 12 BALLPOINT
PENS, BOX CUTTER,
TRAVEL CLOCK, *FLIP
CHART POWER*

TIPS

≋ Purchase materials at office and art supply stores.

≋ Survival kits are a necessity if you present frequently. Searching for basic materials at the presentation wastes time and detracts from the overall flow of the presentation.

≋ A survival kit container needs to be sturdy, easy to open and close, and, of course, big enough for all of your supplies.

≋ Add or subtract from the above list to suit your own needs. Other presenters have found the following items to be helpful: straight pins, pencils, a pencil sharpener, correction tape, double-sided tape, a 12" ruler, chalk, breath spray, and aspirin.

COLOR

Tips

Visibility and Appeal

- The most visible colors are black, blue, and green, in that order.

- Blue and red are the most appealing colors.

- Red is better as an accent color than as a primary color.

- Avoid brown, pink, and yellow for general printing.

Emphasis and Order

- Two colors are more effective than one.

- Use bright colors to add accents or to help organize.
  Example: black with red accents.

- Use contrasting colors for bullets, underlines, arrows, and borders; sub-items in a bulleted list provide an appropriate place to change color.

- Using three colors is acceptable, but it can be confusing to readers.

LETTERS AND WORDS

Tips

- ⚡ Uppercase block letters are easiest for participants to see.

- ⚡ Keep your handwriting consistent in slant and style.

- ⚡ Alternate colors that contrast well to help show where one concept ends and another begins.

- ⚡ Write only essential words to provide a visual aid that reinforces your key points.

- ⚡ Limit yourself to a few key ideas per page.

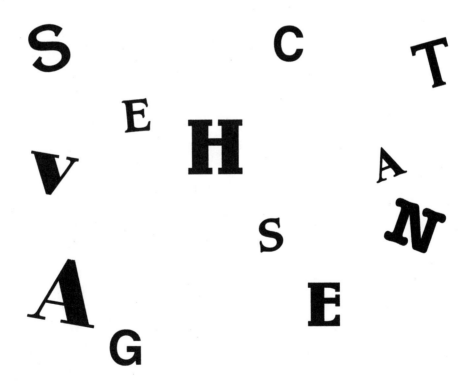

Bullets

Tips

※ Bullets highlight specific points or differentiate one item from another.

※ Using bullets for a list of items, rather than numerals, helps to avoid the illusion that item #1 is more important than item #5.

※ Bullets are usually round dots, but other options include asterisks, squares, arrows, and dashes.

※ For neat and clear presentations, limit how many different types of bullets you use.

※ Indent sub-items and distinguish them from the main points with a different bullet.

※ The size of the bullets depends on the size of the letters on the flip chart; bullets should not be more than one-half the letter size.

Shapes

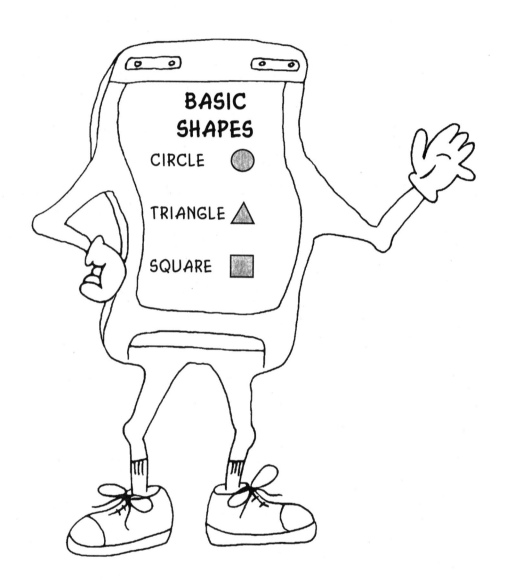

Text inside image: BASIC SHAPES / CIRCLE / TRIANGLE / SQUARE

TIPS

❧ Circles can be made into pictures.
   Examples: sun, face, clock, bag of money

❧ Triangles can be made into symbols.
   Examples: arrow (line added), star (several triangles)

❧ Squares can be made into equipment and objects.
   Examples: building, computer, truck, book

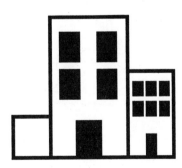

Pictures

Tips

Purpose

- ≋ Pictures and shapes are easier to identify and recall than words or details.

- ≋ Use shapes to create outlines.

- ≋ Pictures need only to be recognizable, not perfect.

- ≋ Avoid too much detail in pictures (in figures and in background).

≢ Pictures are a simple way to display messages.

Pictographs

≢ Pictographs are pictures used to illustrate concrete objects. They are built on basic shapes: circles, triangles, and squares.

Examples:

CIRCLE   SQUARE

Ideographs

≢ Ideographs are pictures that illustrate abstract ideas. They are built on basic shapes: circles, triangles, and squares.

Examples:

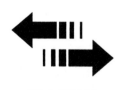

PROGRESS   CREATIVITY   COMMITMENT

Technical Pictures

≋ In technical presentations, you may need a more realistic image (e.g., a circuit board or a skeleton). Suggestions:
- use clip art and enlarge the image
- trace the item from a trade publication
- have an artist draw the image

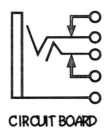

CIRCUIT BOARD

Balance

Tips

≉ Write a specific topic at the top of each flip chart to help participants follow the discussion.

≉ White (blank) space around the copy keeps a flip chart organized, clean, and easy to read.

≉ Leave at least 3" to 4" margins on both sides of the copy. If your points are short, leave even wider margins.

≉ The page will look better if the margin at the bottom of the page is larger than the margin at the top of the page.

Preparation

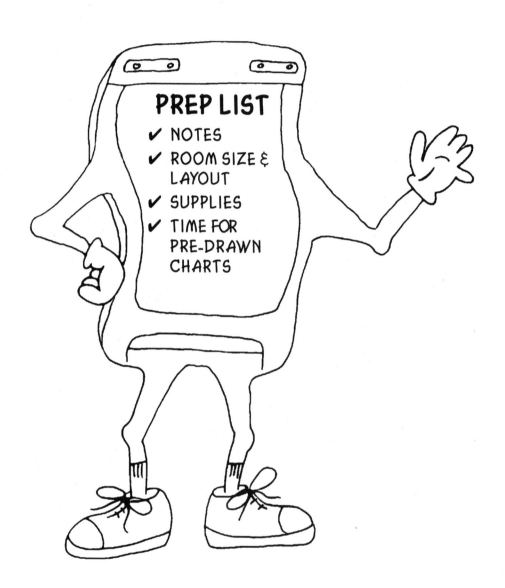

Tips

♨ Reproduce flip charts, word for word, in your presentation notes. During the presentation, you can glance at your presentation notes to see your next point while participants are looking at a flip chart.

♨ Inspect the presentation room yourself. Is it large enough for 1, 2, or more flip chart stands?

♨ Place flip chart stands where participants can view them easily.

♨ Be sure you have enough flip charts, markers, and correction materials.

♨ The time required to make pre-drawn flip charts will depend on how many you are going to make, how much content and detail is involved, and your own level of comfort in doing flip charts.

♨ Leave blank pages between your pre-drawn flip charts.

Fixing Mistakes

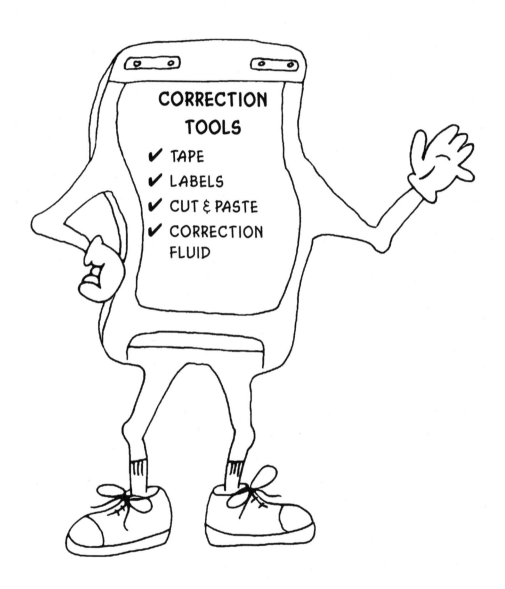

CORRECTION
TOOLS
✔ TAPE
✔ LABELS
✔ CUT & PASTE
✔ CORRECTION
FLUID

Tips

- Tape comes in various widths; 1/6", 1/3", and 5/6" sizes are common. Tape over the mistake and print on the tape.

- Cover-up tape (1" width) can be used to cover mistakes and is easy to write over.

- Labels also come in various sizes. Place a label over the mistake and print on the label.

- To cut out a mistake, put a small piece of cardboard under the page where the mistake was made. Use a box-cutter (single-edged razor) to cut out the error. Remove the cardboard and tape the edges of the flip chart page to the sheet underneath. Write the correct copy in the newly created space.

- Correction fluid (e.g., Liquid Paper®) works well to cover small mistakes. Rewrite the copy after the correction fluid dries.

TIME-SAVING TIPS

TIPS

※ For pre-drawn flip charts, write only the words that are essential for meaning. For spontaneous flip charts, list a participant's key words, which usually occur at the beginning or at the end of his or her comments.

※ Use common abbreviations for all flip charts.
Examples: Employee = EE, With = W/

※ Omit vowels.
Examples: Develop = DVLP, Manager = MNGR

※ Truncate (cut off the ends of words).
Examples: Problem = PROB, Objective = OBJ

※ Handwriting that is in all capital letters and that has the same slant is easiest for participants to read.

STORING YOUR MASTERPIECES

TIPS

≋ Roll your charts under (i.e., print side out). This prevents them from curling up on the easel when you next use them. Use tape or rubber bands to secure the roll. Write the topic and date on an outside corner in small print.

≋ Office and art supply stores sell racks that can hang up to 12 flip chart pads.

≋ Office and art supply stores sell flat cabinets that are excellent for preserving flip charts. Drawer labels allow charts to be located easily.

Travel Carriers

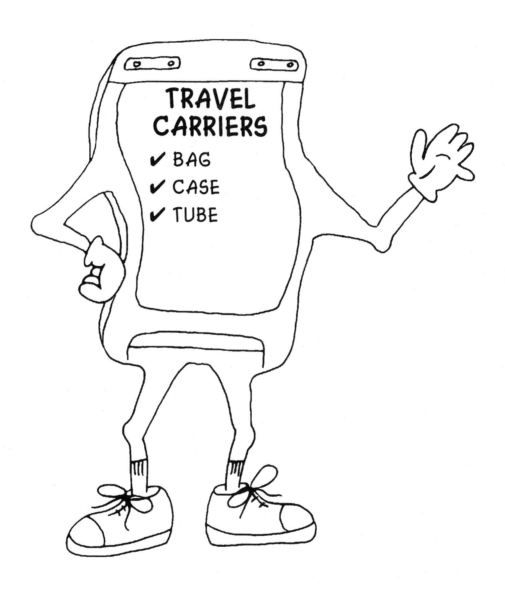

Tips

⚡ Bags range from large plastic trash bags to vinyl or leather bags. Bags are a good option if the materials are not going to be moved often.

⚡ The most common cases are made of fiberboard or reinforced leatherette, providing more protection than bags.

⚡ Rigid tubes offer the most protection. A thick cardboard or plastic tube is both light and easy to handle. Attaching straps adds to the ease of travel.

KEY POINTS

Paper

Flip chart pad (27" x 34"): blank or with blue grids, approximately 60 sheets, holes at the top for hanging
Newsprint sheets (12" x 18" or 18" x 24"): approximately 100 sheets, spiral bound and/or perforated

Markers

Water color markers: popular, bright colors, chisel tip, scented (optional)

Tape

Scotch™ general purpose-masking tape, 1"

Stand

Easel: sturdy, back plate
Tripod: easily portable, no back plate

Use of Color

Color provides emphasis and visibility, shows order, and is visually appealing.
Use combinations of colors that contrast well: red and black, red and blue, or green and black.

Letters and Words

Print letters in all CAPITALS, alternate colors after segments of content, use key words only, and write a maximum of 7 ideas per sheet.

Bullets

Use bullets to highlight specific points or to differentiate one item from another.

Shapes

Use the basics (circles, triangles, and squares) to create pictures and symbols.

Pictures

Use simple pictures to relay ideas and concepts.

Balance

Leave sufficient white space and margins around the copy.

Survival Kit

Includes 1" masking tape, markers, scissors, glue stick, transparent tape, hole punch, stapler, paper clips, rubber bands, pens, box cutter, travel clock, and *Flip Chart Power*

Preparation

Check room size, layout, and supplies.

Fixing Mistakes

Use self-adhesive tape, labels, cut and paste, or correction fluid.

Time-Saving Tips

Key words only
Abbreviate
Settle on a style

Storing

Roll
Hang
Lay flat

Carrier

Bag
Case
Tube

QUICK CHECK

Instructions: Circle T if the statement is true.
Circle F if the statement is false.

1. T F   Grid lines on flip charts help you to print in straight lines.

2. T F   Markers come in different sizes, shapes, and point sizes.

3. T F   All masking tapes have the same adhesiveness.

4. T F   A flip chart easel is sturdier than a tripod.

5. T F   A survival kit should have scissors.

6. T F   Words should be printed in upper and lowercase letters.

7. T F   People remember shapes more easily than words.

8. T F   Before you present, be sure to check the room size, layout, and your supplies.

9. T F   If you make a writing mistake on a flip chart, you have to start all over.

10. T F   A presenter should not abbreviate words.

11. T F   Flip charts can be stored by rolling, hanging, or laying flat.

12. T F   The most common flip chart carriers are bags, cases, and tubes.

NOTES

QUICK CHECK ANSWERS

1. (T) F   Grid lines on flip charts help you to print in straight lines. (p. 61)

2. (T) F   Markers come in different sizes, shapes, and point sizes. (p. 63)

3. T (F)   All masking tapes have the same adhesiveness. (p. 65)

4. (T) F   A flip chart easel is sturdier than a tripod. (p. 66)

5. (T) F   A survival kit should have scissors. (p. 68)

6. T (F)   Words should be printed in upper and lowercase letters. (p. 72)

7. (T) F   People remember shapes more easily than words. (p. 79)

8. (T) F   Before you present, be sure to check the room size, layout, and your supplies. (p. 85)

9. T (F)   If you make a writing mistake on a flip chart, you have to start all over. (p. 87)

10. T (F)   A presenter should not abbreviate words. (p. 89)

11. (T) F   Flip charts can be stored by rolling, hanging, or laying flat. (p. 90)

12. (T) F   The most common flip chart carriers are bags, cases, and tubes. (p. 92)

PRESENTING FLIP CHARTS

Facing the Audience

TIPS

≋ Be sure you are facing the audience while referring to flip charts. Participants can hear you better and will be able to see your facial expressions.

≋ Stand to the side when writing on a flip chart. (If you are right-handed, stand with the flip chart on your left; if you are left-handed, stand with the flip chart on your right.) It may be more difficult for you, but participants appreciate seeing what you are writing. This also helps to speed up participants' reading and processing time.

POINTING

Tips

❧ Directing the participants as to where to look does the following:
- Reinforces key ideas
- Helps participants to stay focused
- Encourages continual interaction and involvement

❧ As you begin a topic, point to the related copy or picture on the flip chart.
- You can use a pointer, a marker, or your hand.
- In a formal group, use a pointer.
- In an informal group, use a marker or your hand to point.

Moving Around

TIPS

- Hold a marker in one hand and use the other hand to turn the flip chart pages.

- Walk around and observe participants' progress during group activities. This also provides support to participants.

- If you have 2 flip charts available, move between them.

PRESENTING ON A FRONT AND BACK STAGE

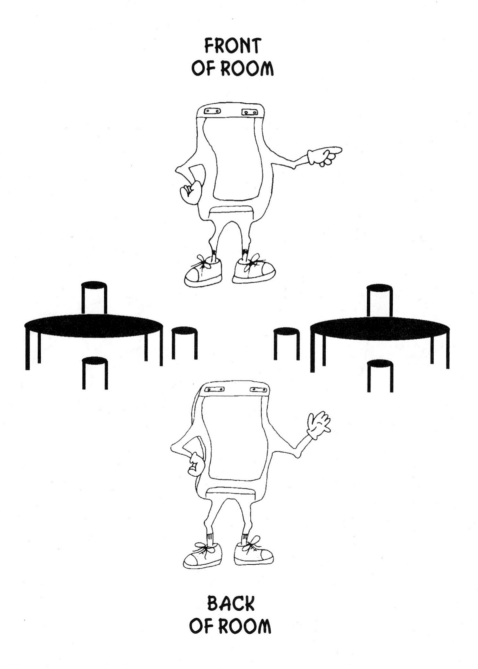

FRONT
OF ROOM

BACK
OF ROOM

Tips

❧ Use this technique in the following way:
  - List one topic on a flip chart at the front of the room. List another topic on another flip chart at the back of the room.
  - After you finish the topic at the front of the room, walk to the back of the room and present the topic on the second flip chart.

❧ This technique changes the pace of your presentation.

❧ Physically shifting the presentation focus helps to keep those participants who are sitting in the back of the room more involved.

❧ Because you are doing something out of the ordinary, you inspire more creative thinking from the participants.

Tripping and Recovering

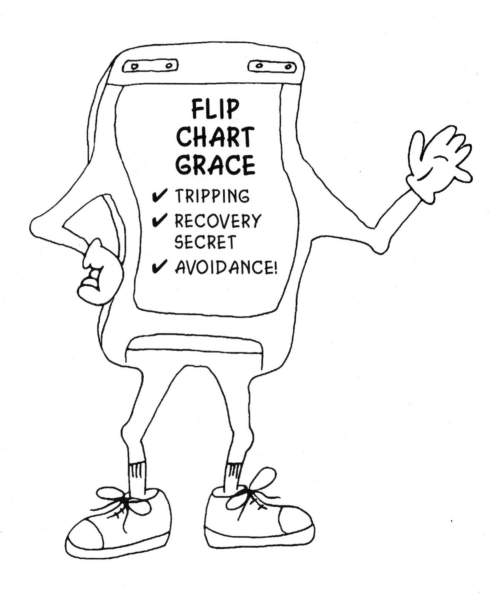

TIPS

Tripping: Who me?

≉ It is easy to get involved in a discussion, hear a great idea, and want to race to the flip chart to write it down, not realizing you are right in front of the flip chart. You step back and boom; you meet the flip chart!

Recovery secret

≉ A sense of humor is a must! Comments like "Anybody else see that flip chart attack me?" help set you and the participants at ease.

Avoidance: Suggestions (No guarantees!)

≉ Place the stand near the front wall, leaving more space between you and participants.

≉ Set the stand parallel to the front wall, not at an angle.

≉ Use a flip chart easel rather than a tripod. (An easel is usually sturdier.)

Writing Gracefully at the Bottom of a Page

TIPS

- Slide the flip chart sheet up to a comfortable level for writing.

- Tip the flip chart stand away from you.

- Pull the pad and its backing away from the flip chart stand. Support the pad with one hand while you write with the other.

- Kneel down and print.

- As a last resort, bend over and print.

Keeping Your Place

Tips

≋ Synchronizing the flip chart message and your verbal message creates clarity for the participants and adds to your credibility as a presenter.

≋ Turn each flip chart page after you finish discussing its contents.

≋ To turn a page smoothly, grab a bottom corner of the flip chart sheet. Pull the sheet up, holding it close to the pad itself. Lead the sheet over the top of the flip chart stand.

SELECTING THE CORRECT FLIP CHART PAGE EVERY TIME

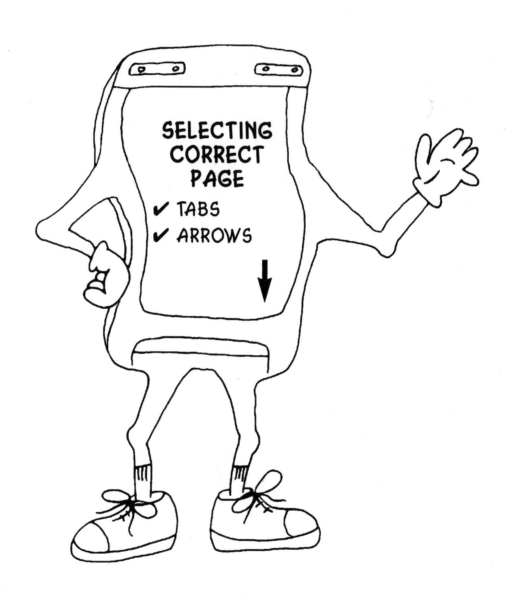

TIPS

❧ Put a tab, made by folding over a piece of masking tape, on the flip chart sheet. Mark the tab with a number, a word, or some other type of identifier.

If several sheets need to be labeled, start the tabs at the bottom of the first sheet and progress upward on subsequent sheets.

❧ Draw arrows on the flip charts themselves, especially when you are using more than one flip chart stand.

An arrow on the current flip chart page will indicate where your next chart can be found. For example, an arrow pointing to the right indicates that your next page is on the easel to the right; an arrow pointing down means the next page is on the same easel.

Making Notes

Tips

⚡ Write lightly penciled notes to yourself on the flip chart.

⚡ Write notes big enough so that you can read them easily during your presentation (approximately 1/2" high).

⚡ Write only key words intended to trigger your memory.

⚡ Place notes high on the sheet, separating different ideas with about 2" of white space. Avoid placing notes directly next to related points on pre-drawn sheets; it is awkward to bend over and read them.

Exception: If you want to pencil in notes as templates that can be drawn over during the presentation, place the pencil notes in the appropriate places on the flip chart page. For example, to illustrate an acronym, you might pre-draw the letters of the acronym in marker and the remaining letters of each word in pencil. Then, during the presentation, you can easily and neatly write what the acronym stands for.

Using More Than One Easel

(Flip Chart #1)

(Flip Chart #2)

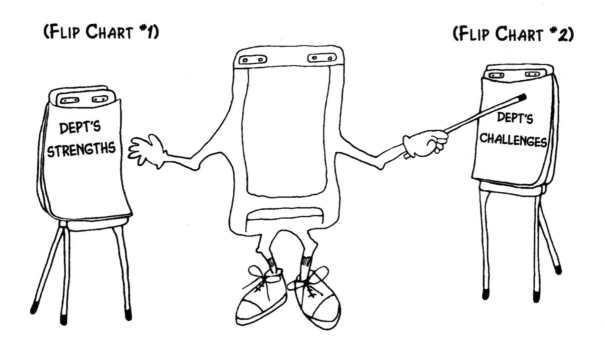

Tips

Using Two Flip Charts

≋ Select 2 categories related to same overall subject and list each one on a separate flip chart (e.g., "Dept's Strengths" and "Dept's Challenges").

≋ Have the flip chart you are going to use first on the participants' left. Place the second flip chart a few feet to the right.

≋ Begin your presentation or discussion and solicit ideas from participants.

≋ Be sure to record the responses on the appropriate flip chart.

Keeping Track

≋ Number the stands by putting a small piece of masking tape on the side edge of each stand. Put the tape near the top, in the same place on each stand. Write #1 on the tape on the stand you will use first and then number the other stands according to their sequence of use.

≋ Standardize the position of certain repetitive flip charts.

Examples:

• If using 2 stands, use the one on the left for pre-drawn flip charts and the one on the right for spontaneous writing during the meeting.

• If using 3 stands, use the first stand for the agenda, the second stand for objectives, and the third stand for the summary.

• Always work your way across 2 or 3 stands. The first chart should be on the first stand, the second chart on the second stand, the third chart on the third stand, and the fourth chart back on the first stand. Make sure that the flow will work for your session.

Using a Video Screen

Tips

- The flip chart stand should have center stage. Too often the video screen is placed right in the middle of the flip charts, even though the video may only take 5 minutes. Do not let the video presentation determine the setup for your whole session.

- Place the video screen to the side of the flip chart stand, not in the middle of the room.

- Ask the participants to position themselves so they can see the video screen. When the video is over, move the screen out of the way.

KEY POINTS

Facing the Audience

Be sure you are facing the participants as you refer to the flip chart pages. When writing, stand to the side and write.

Pointing

As you present a topic, point to the related copy or picture on the flip chart. Use a pointer, a marker, or your hand.

Moving Around

Hold a marker in one hand to prevent yourself from holding on to the flip chart stand. During the presentation, find ways to take at least a few steps away from the flip chart.

Presenting at the Front and Back

Using two flip charts placed at different places in the room allows you to incorporate movement into your presentation and encourages creativity from participants.

Tripping and Recovering

Place the stand near the front wall so there is more space between you and participants. Set the stand parallel to the front wall, not at an angle. If you do trip, be sure to maintain your sense of humor.

Writing at the Bottom of a Page

Slide the sheet up, tip the stand away from you, pick up the bottom of the pad and its backing, kneel down, or just bend over and write.

Keeping Your Place

Flip each sheet when you are finished talking about its contents.

Turning a Page Gracefully

Grab a bottom corner of the sheet and pull the sheet up, holding it close to the pad. Lead the sheet over the top of the stand.

Selecting the Correct Page

Place masking tape tabs on the flip chart sheets. Mark the tabs with numbers, words, or some other identifiers.

Making Notes on a Flip Chart

Write lightly with pencil, high on the flip chart page, using only key words.

Using More Than One Easel

This technique allows for easy comparisons between topics and provides participants the opportunity to see all the salient points of several topics at once. Number the stands or standardize their positions, or work your way across 2 or 3 stands.

Using a Video Screen

Put the flip chart stands in the front center of the room and place the video screen to one side. Ask participants to reposition themselves as necessary when it is time for them to view the video.

QUICK CHECK

Instructions: Write the missing word in the blank space.

1. When you present, face the _____.

2. When you point, it helps the participants _____ _____ _____.

3. Rather than standing by the flip chart stand during the whole presentation, it is better to _____ _____.

4. If you do trip over your flip chart stand, it helps to have a _____ of _____.

5. One way to write at the bottom of the page is to slide the _____ up.

6. When you are done talking about a sheet's contents, you should _____ the sheet.

7. It is best to turn a page by grabbing a bottom _____.

8. You can use _____ _____ to create tabs for your flip charts.

9. A _____ is the best writing tool for making notes on your flip chart.

10. One technique for using more than one flip chart is to _____ the stands.

11. If you are only showing a video for a few minutes, then place the screen _____ _____ _____.

NOTES

QUICK CHECK ANSWERS

1. When you present, face the <u>audience</u>. (p. 101)

2. When you point, it helps the participants <u>to</u> <u>stay</u> <u>focused</u>. (p. 103)

3. Rather than standing by the flip chart stand during the whole presentation, it is better to <u>move</u> <u>around</u>. (p. 104)

4. If you do trip over your flip chart stand, it helps to have a <u>sense</u> of <u>humor</u>. (p. 109)

5. One way to write at the bottom of the page is to slide the <u>sheet</u> up. (p. 111)

6. When you are done talking about a sheet's contents, you should <u>turn</u> the sheet. (p. 113)

7. It is best to turn a page by grabbing a bottom <u>corner</u>. (p. 113)

8. You can use <u>masking</u> <u>tape</u> to create tabs for your flip charts. (p. 115)

9. A <u>pencil</u> is the best writing tool for making notes on your flip chart. (p. 117)

10. One technique for using more than one flip chart is to <u>number</u> the stands. (p. 119)

11. If you are only showing a video for a few minutes, then place the screen <u>to</u> <u>the</u> <u>side</u>. (p. 121)

APPENDIX

OTHER PRESENTATION TOOLS

Advantages	Tools	Concerns
✔ Can be prepared in advance. ✔ Images are in color. ✔ Information can be added. ✔ Projected image can be seen throughout room.	✔ Transparencies 1-100 participants	✔ Projectors can be loud and hot. ✔ Overhead arm can block participants' view. ✔ Bulbs can burn out. ✔ Presenters tend to read from screen.
✔ Inexpensive. ✔ Erase easily. ✔ Lights on—audience stays involved. ✔ Flexible—promotes audience interaction.	✔ Whiteboards (Dry Erase Boards) or Chalkboards 1-25 participants	✔ Chalk limits contrast and visibility. ✔ Chalkboard can be dirty and dusty. ✔ Whiteboard requires special erasable markers. ✔ Limit predrawn material.
✔ High-quality, professional image. ✔ Can use color for impact. ✔ Consistent message can be presented to many audiences. ✔ Portable.	✔ Slides 1-200 participants	✔ Preparation can be time consuming and expensive. ✔ Equipment can be loud. ✔ Dark room limits interaction and eye contact. ✔ Prepared sequence limits spontaneity.
✔ Immediate feedback. ✔ Can be replayed as needed. ✔ Good library of subjects available. ✔ Allows for multiscreen capability.	✔ Videotapes 1-25 participants per monitor	✔ Amateur videotaping can be of poor quality. ✔ Professional videotape rental can be expensive. ✔ Small screens. ✔ Impersonal—can inhibit interaction with participants.

Adapted with the permission of APICS, Inc. *Train the Trainer: Building Block of Education,* 1991, p. 7-4.

Transparency Users: Bonus Tips

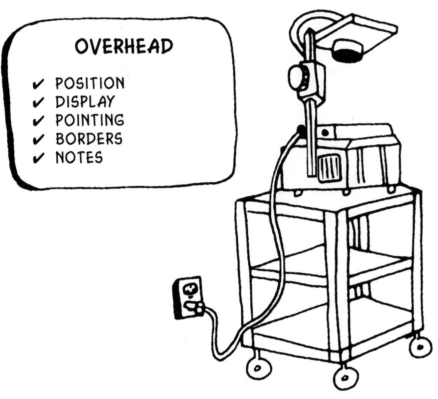

OVERHEAD

✔ POSITION
✔ DISPLAY
✔ POINTING
✔ BORDERS
✔ NOTES

Position

❧ Use a frame on the projector surface to position your transparencies in place. You can buy a frame or you can create your own. One simple way to make a frame is to cut cardboard into 1"-wide strips. Then use masking tape to attach strips to the projector surface.

Display

❧ When you are not using the overhead projector during your presentation, shut it off. (The bright light is hard on participants' eyes.)

❧ To display only a portion of a transparency, cover the remainder of it with a sheet of heavy paper.

❧ To emphasize a point or to encourage group involvement, use overhead markers (e.g., Sanford® Vis-a-Vis) to write on the transparencies. Alternatively, to preserve the original transparency, place a clear transparency over the original transparency and write the added information on the clear one.

POINTING

- ⚡ If you are pointing at the screen, use a long screen pointer or a ruler, not your hand.

- ⚡ If you are pointing to the transparency itself, use a short pointer: a pen or marker works very well.

BORDERS

- ⚡ Premade borders add a professional look to transparencies. You can purchase borders that attach permanently to your transparencies.

- ⚡ The most common borders are made of white cardboard (e.g., 3M brand Paperboard Transparency Mounting Frames). Put one border on each side of each transparency and tape the borders together.

NOTES

- ⚡ Use the borders on your transparencies to write your presentation notes (use only key words). On each transparency, also note the times during which you plan to be presenting that content (e.g., 9:30-9:40 a.m.).

WHITEBOARD AND CHALKBOARD USERS: BONUS TIPS

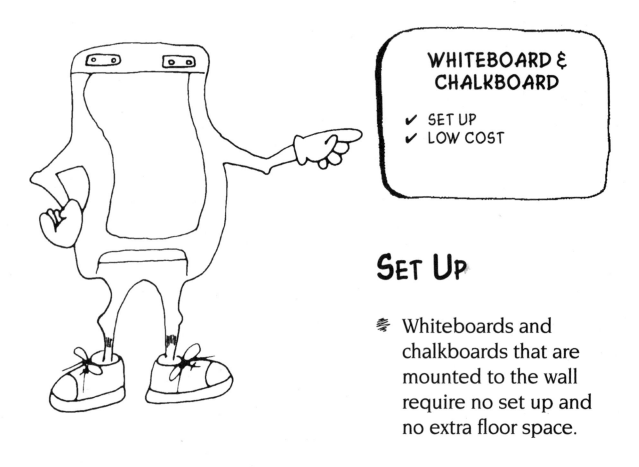

**WHITEBOARD &
CHALKBOARD**

✔ SET UP
✔ LOW COST

SET UP

≋ Whiteboards and chalkboards that are mounted to the wall require no set up and no extra floor space.

LOW COST

≋ Using whiteboards or chalkboards eliminates the costs of flip chart paper, water color markers, and tape. However, whiteboards do require special dry erase markers (such as Marks-A-Lot™) and chalkboards require chalk and an eraser.

SLIDE USERS: BONUS TIPS

SEQUENCE AND POSITION

> ⚡ View all your slides prior to your presentation to check the sequence and the slide direction.

```
┌─────────────────────────┐
│      SLIDE USERS         │
│                          │
│  ✔ SEQUENCE/POSITION     │
│  ✔ EQUIPMENT             │
│    CHECK/PRACTICE         │
│  ✔ ASSISTANCE            │
│                          │
└─────────────────────────┘
```

EQUIPMENT CHECK AND PRACTICE

> ⚡ Check that the slide projector is functioning properly and practice with the equipment before your presentation. In particular, you will want to review the following:
> - Do you know how to turn the machine on and off?
> - Do you know how to progress through the slides?
> - Is the screen in the correct position?
> - Is the image clear?
> - Have you made arrangements to darken the room?

ASSISTANCE

> ⚡ If someone will be assisting you in presenting the slide show, practice together in advance so that he or she will be familiar with the timing of the presentation and will know exactly when to advance the slides.

Videotape Users: Bonus Tips

Practice

≋ Before your session, be sure that you know how to operate the videocassette recorder (VCR). Practice turning it on and inserting and playing your tape.

Cue Up

≋ Before the session, set the videotape to the point at which you want to begin.

≋ Plan ahead and show only the segments of the videotape that are pertinent to the participants.

Volume

≋ Ask participants to let you know whether or not the volume is loud enough.

Resources

Books

The Big Yellow Drawing Book by Dan O'Neil, Marion O'Neil, and Hugh D. O'Neil, Jr. Published by Hugh O'Neil & Associates, Nevada City, CA, 1974.

Effective Presentation Skills by International Training Corporation. Published by Pfeiffer & Company, San Diego, CA, 1993.

Fearless and Flawless Public Speaking with Power, Polish, and Pizazz by Mary-Ellen Drummond. Published by Pfeiffer & Company, San Diego, CA, 1993.

Field Guide to Flip Charts by Jean Westcott and Jennifer Hammond Landau, 1987. Available from Jean Westcott and Jennifer Hammond Landau, 1032 Bay View Avenue, Oakland, CA 94610, (510) 536-1657.

Flip Charts: How to Draw Them and How to Use Them by Richard C. Brandt. Published by Pfeiffer & Company, San Diego, CA, 1986.

Fundamentals of Graphic Language: Practice Book (2nd ed.) by David Sibbet. Published by Grove Consultants International, San Francisco, CA, 1993.

Graphics for Presenters by Lynn Kearny. Published by Crisp Publications, Menlo Park, CA, 1995.

I See What You Mean by David Sibbet. Published by Grove Consultants International, San Francisco, CA, 1981.

Instructional Technology: Foundations by Robert M. Gagne. Published by Lawrence Erlbaum Associates, Hillsdale, NJ, 1987.

A Picture's Worth 1000 Words by Jean Westcott and Jennifer Hammond Landau, 1993. Available from Jean Westcott and Jennifer Hammond Landau, 1032 Bay View Avenue, Oakland, CA 94610, (510) 536-1657.

Point, Click, and Wow!! by Claudyne Wilder and David Fine. Published by Pfeiffer & Company, San Diego, CA, 1996.

"Presentation Skills with Visual Aids" from *20 Active Training Programs* by Mel Silberman. Published by Pfeiffer & Company, San Diego, CA, 1992.

Seminars

Creating High Impact Visuals and Interactive Learning Activities. Robert W. Pike, CSP, Creative Training Techniques International, Inc., 7620 West 78th Street, Edina, MN 55439, (800) 383-9210

The Fundamentals of Group Graphics Workshop. Grove Consultants International, 832 Folsom, San Francisco, CA 94107, (415) 882-7760

Get Graphic! How to Create Visuals That Work Lynn Kearny, Performance Management Consultant, 5379 Broadway, Oakland, CA 94618, (510) 547-1896

Visual Communication for Training and Consulting. Jean Westcott and Jennifer Hammond Landau, 1032 Bay View Avenue, Oakland, CA 94610, (510) 536-1657

INDEX